7 Leadership Lessons to Foster a Culture of Care

A Leaders Blue Book for Supporting and Empowering Post Partum Moms in the Workforce

CORAETTA
ANDRENA

Dedication

I dedicate this book to several remarkable individuals who have deeply impacted my journey.

First, to a woman I will call Kate, who rushed to be by my side during one of my darkest moments. Kate, you taught me the invaluable lesson of self-advocacy—never be afraid to ask for what you deserve and listening to your own body during pregnancy. Your unwavering support and wisdom have left an imprint on my heart, and for that, I am forever grateful.

Next, to my sons—you are my world! If you ever read this book, know that the experiences I share throughout these pages made me a stronger, better version of myself for you. Each loss I endured brought me closer to the incredible joy of meeting you, holding you, and witnessing your first smiles. I wouldn't change any of my experiences because they led me to you. When the time comes for you and your future partners to embark on the journey of parenthood, I hope you will be patient, kind, and understanding. You never know how rough that journey might be, but it will be worth every moment.

CORAETTA ANDRENA

Table Of Contents

01 — Empathy First: The Importance of Compassionate Leadership — 8
Understanding and acknowledging the unique challenges faced by Soldiers experiencing pregnancy and postpartum, including those who have lost a baby

02 — Active Listening: Creating a Safe Space for Open Communication — 15
Encouraging Soldiers to share their experiences and feelings without fear of judgement or repercussions

03 — Recognizing the Signs: Early Detection of Emotional and Physical Struggles — 26
Training Leaders to identify the signs of postpartum depression, anxiety, and grief to provide timely support

04 — Supportive Policies: Implementing Family-Friendly Practices — 39
Developing and enforcing policies that support Soldiers during pregnancy and postpartum, such as flexible leave and accommodations; Understanding how delicate the womb is during the 1st trimester

05 — Resource Awareness: Connecting Soldiers with Professional Help — 47
Ensuring Leaders are knowledgeable about available resources, including mental health services, support groups, and medical care

06 — Creating a Community: Fostering Peer Support Networks — 55
Encouraging the development of support groups and peer mentoring to help Soldiers feel less isolated and more understood

07 — Continual Education: Ongoing Training and Development for Leaders — 62
Providing regular training on the latest research and best practices for supporting Soldiers through pregnancy, postpartum, and loss to maintain a culture of care

Table Of Contents (cont.)

Final Reflections   67

About the Author   72

Cited Quotations   77

Resources   78

Preface

This book was born out of a journey filled with love, loss, resilience, and the unwavering commitment to serve others. As an African American woman, a retired combat veteran with over two decades of service, and a mother who has faced the unimaginable pain of losing a child, my life has been a tapestry woven with threads of both triumph and tragedy. This book is my way of sharing the lessons I've learned, the strength I've found, and the hope I hold for a future where every Soldier feels seen, heard, and supported.

Throughout my military career, I witnessed the extraordinary courage of Soldiers on the battlefield, but I also saw the silent battles fought in the hearts and minds of those who faced challenges that were not as easily visible. Pregnancy, miscarriage, and the loss of a child are among the most profound struggles a person can endure, and yet, these experiences are often met with silence or misunderstanding within the ranks. The Army, with its focus on mission readiness and resilience, sometimes overlooks the emotional and psychological needs of its Soldiers, particularly those dealing with pregnancy-related issues.

CORAETTA ANDRENA

Preface

This book is not just a recounting of my personal experiences; it is a call to action for leaders at every level. It is a guide to fostering a culture of care, empathy, and understanding within our military. I believe that by sharing my story and the stories of others, we can change the way the Army approaches the care of its Soldiers, especially those navigating the complexities of pregnancy and loss.

My journey has been marked by six pregnancies, each one teaching me something new about myself and the world around me. I have two living children who are my greatest joy, but I have also experienced the heartbreak of three miscarriages and the indescribable pain of losing a son who lived for only two hours after being born prematurely. These experiences have shaped me into the woman and Leader I am today, and they have fueled my passion for advocating for better support systems within the military.

As a senior leader in the Army, I often found myself in positions of great responsibility, making decisions that affected the lives of those under my command. But it wasn't until I faced my own personal tragedies that I truly understood the importance of

CORAETTA ANDRENA

Preface

leading with empathy and compassion. This book is my way of giving back to the military community that has been such a significant part of my life. It is my hope that the lessons shared here will resonate with Leaders and Soldiers alike, and that together, we can create an environment where every Soldier feels valued and supported. The pages that follow are filled with hard truths, valuable lessons, and a vision for a better future. They are a testament to the strength of the human spirit and the power of community.

Whether you are a Soldier, a Leader, or someone who cares deeply about the well-being of those who serve, I invite you to join me on this journey. Together, we can make a difference in the lives of our Soldiers, ensuring that they never have to walk through their struggles alone.

CORAETTA ANDRENA

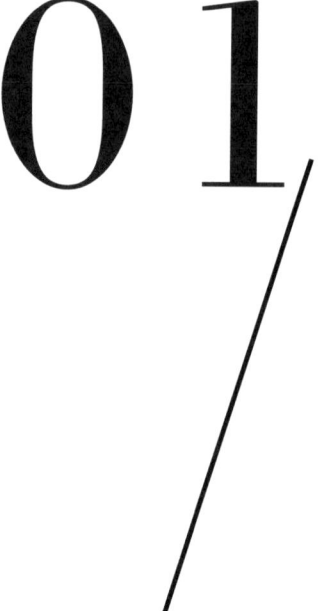

LESSON

7 LEADERSHIP LESSONS

Lesson One:

Empathy First - The Importance of Compassionate Leadership

Empathy is the foundation of effective leadership, especially when dealing with the complex and deeply personal experiences of Soldiers undergoing pregnancy, postpartum, and, in some cases, loss. Understanding and compassion are not just supportive actions; they are essential qualities that Leaders must cultivate to foster a culture of care. This chapter explores the significance of empathy in leadership, using a personal narrative to illustrate its critical role.

A Personal Experience: Learning Empathy Through Loss

In the early morning hours, I found myself leading a physical training session at Loyola University, where I served as a Professor of Military Science. The morning was typical for a training session, filled with the rhythmic cadence of exercises and the camaraderie of Soldiers working together. As we progressed through the session, performing iron mikes from one yard line to the next, everything seemed routine.

After the workout, I returned to our makeshift office—a repurposed old house on campus designated for the ROTC program. This space had become familiar, a place where we could unwind and prepare for the day's academic and administrative responsibilities. I headed to the bathroom, expecting to carry on with my usual post-PT routine. However, as I squatted over the toilet, I noticed blood in my underwear. A wave of confusion and concern washed over me. It was my first pregnancy, and I had no reference point for what was normal. Trying to remain calm, I cleaned myself up and decided to seek medical attention.

I went to the office of my superior, a white male LTC, and informed him of my situation, expressing the need to go to the hospital. His response was immediate and supportive, urging me to take care of myself and let him know the outcome. His reaction provided a much-needed sense of reassurance and understanding, a clear demonstration of compassionate leadership in action.

Driving through the busy streets of Baltimore, I arrived at Mercy Medical Center, filled with a mix of hope and fear. After checking in at the Emergency Room, I was seen by a doctor who, given the early stage of my pregnancy, chose to conduct a manual examination rather than an ultrasound. As I waited in hesitation to learn where the blood had come from, I watched the nurse set up all of the instruments for the doctor. I tried not to worry and await the news. After the nurse completed setting things up, the doctor proceeded with his examination. As with any other vaginal examination I remained tense and before I knew it, the doctor was complete and sliding back in his chair to remove his gloves. He then went over to the sink to wash his hands. He then turned to me and my husband at the time to deliver the news to us. The news was delivered with clinical precision—I had miscarried. The moment was surreal and numbing. I was left grappling with a whirlwind of emotions, unsure of how to process them or whether I even had the right to mourn the loss so early in the pregnancy.

In that moment, I did not shed a tear. I sat up on the bed and proceeded with cleaning myself off from the gels left on my inner thigh from the examination. Once I cleaned up, we waited for the nurse to return with the discharge papers and my husband and I left the hospital that day in complete disbelief. The drive home was quiet. Neither of us uttered a word.

Lessons in Empathy and Leadership

This experience taught me invaluable lessons about empathy and the role of Leadership in supporting Soldiers through personal crises. As a leader, my superior's compassionate response was a lifeline. It reminded me that empathy isn't just about understanding someone else's feelings; it's about taking action to support and validate their experiences. His simple yet sincere concern provided comfort during an incredibly vulnerable moment.

General Ann E. Dunwoody said it best, "the best leaders are those who listen with an open mind, who lead with their heart, and who inspire their team to achieve their greatest potential." My LTC at that time, did not understand, in that moment what I could have been feeling inside due to the sudden onset of blood, but he did not shun me off nor criticize me to believe my situation was not important. He embraced my concern with an open mind and encouraged me to leave duty so that I could seek medical treatment. He knew I had a class to teach that morning and the cadets were counting on me. As a leader, he did not get emotional, but he did exhibit a heart of concern toward my situation and that left me forever grateful to him.

For leaders in the military, fostering a culture of care requires more than policies and procedures; it demands a genuine commitment to understanding and addressing the personal challenges Soldiers face. Whether dealing with pregnancy, postpartum issues, or the loss of a child, Leaders must recognize these experiences' profound emotional and psychological impact. Empathy enables Leaders to create a safe and supportive environment where Soldiers feel seen, heard, and cared for, regardless of the severity or visibility of their struggles.

By sharing my story, I hope to emphasize the importance of empathy in Leadership. It's a reminder that our Soldiers' well-being extends beyond physical readiness; it encompasses emotional and mental health as well. As we move through this blue book, remember that the most powerful tool a Leader possesses is the ability to listen with empathy and act with compassion. These qualities are not just nice to have; they are essential for creating a supportive and resilient military community.

> *"Leadership* is not about being in charge. *It's* about taking care of those in your charge."

~ Simon Sinek

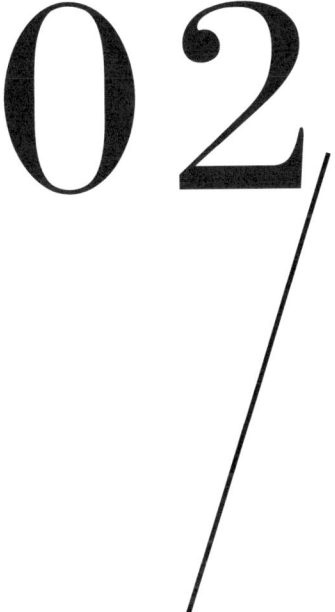

LESSON

Lesson Two:

Active Listening - Creating a Safe Space for Open Communication

Active listening is an essential skill for Leaders, especially when supporting Soldiers through difficult experiences like pregnancy, postpartum, and loss. Creating a safe space for open communication allows individuals to share their stories and feelings without fear of judgment or repercussions. This chapter delves into the importance of active listening and how leaders can cultivate an environment where Soldiers feel heard and supported.

A Personal Experience: The Power of Listening in Times of Loss

The Kat Williams concert in Baltimore, Maryland, was supposed to be a night of laughter and entertainment, a brief escape from the daily grind. My husband and I were looking forward to enjoying the comedy show, but underlying my excitement was a lingering sense of unease. After experiencing a miscarriage previously, I found myself hesitant to go out or be in public for extended periods, often overwhelmed by the fear of something going wrong.

As we settled into our floor seats, guided by an usher's flashlight, the show began. My husband always wanted to enjoy a good laugh. Before the show really got started, he was fully immersed and excited to just be there.Meanwhile, I was happy to be there with him, but I couldn't shake the feeling that something was off. If I bend over a certain way, I felt anxiety about what if I bent the wrong way. If I walked for too long, I felt anxiety as if I maybe was on my feet for too long. So in that arena that day, I worried, what if Kat Williams actually got me to laugh, but what if I laugh too hard. My mind was heavy with worry. My thoughts and anxiety tried to consume me, but I quickly dismissed the negative thoughts and tried to enjoy just being present.

After I got out of my head, I looked over at my husband who seem to not have a care in the world, so I smiled at him and I tried to laugh and participate. After about the first couple of acts on stage, I felt the need to use the restroom. I leaned over to my husband to let him know I would be right back, as I needed to go to the restroom. I jumped out of my seat and turned to head out of the arena and as I stood, the usher that had seated up smiled at me and turned on the flashlight so I could see where I was walking. I politely smiled back and went on my way. I hoped the short walk to the restroom would help calm my nerves. I never expected the inevitable of what would happen next.

Walking out from the arena floor, it was noisy as expected, the lights were dim so everyone could see the person on stage. By the time I reached the corridor, the way was lit up, so I didn't have to squint much longer nor, look down at my feet to make sure I did not trip over anything. The concession stands were open and lines just as long as if the show had just started. I could smell the popcorn and hot dogs cooking up behind the concessions. I could have used a bite to eat, but feeding my belly was the last thing on my mind. I was trying to get to the restroom. Before I knew it, I looked up and I saw the sign to the women's restroom. Walking in, I tried to find the first one open, I felt if I had waited any longer, I probably would have peed on myself.

The arena restroom was typical, with rows of stalls. I chose one that seemed relatively clean and entered in. I quickly turned to the stall door and locked the latch, I checked for toilet paper. That has happened before, getting into a restroom only to realize their was no toilet paper. Luckily for me, their was some in my stall. After I completed all my own quality assurance checks, I pulled down my pants and underwear and squatted over the toilet, a habit ingrained in me since childhood. I never looked down, I was just focused on ensuring I didn't lose my balance and sit on the seat. As I began to relieve myself, I felt a sudden rush and a large clot pass through my uterus. It was a jarring and confusing moment. The clot fell, so fast, into the toilet, and before I could comprehend what had happened, the automatic flush whisked it away. Stunned and scared, I couldn't think. I quickly put on a pad and cleaned up, my mind racing to process the sudden and unexpected event.

Returning to my seat, I felt a mix of fear and uncertainty. I mean, I've felt something like that before, during my menstrual cycles. But that was because I had a history of passing large blood clots while on my period. This time was different, I was not on my period, I was actually pregnant. I could not understand my body. Being new to this pregnancy journey, again I did not understand what was normal and what was not. Still replaying what just happened in my head, I continued to find my way back into the arena and to my seat. I had made it back to my husband, only this time I was wearing a pad. He did not know.

I finally I leaned over to my husband and quietly told him we needed to leave and go to the hospital. He looked at me, confused at first, but when I explained I was bleeding, he immediately understood the urgency. We hurried out of the arena, leaving the sounds of laughter behind. Luckily for me, I had a sweater that I brought with me, just in case I got cold. I used that sweater to drape around the lower part of my body. I was unsure how much blood I was going to lose, and I didn't want to be embarrassed if blood had started seeping through my sweat pants.

We finally made it out of the arena and rushed off to the hospital. My husband kept asking what happened, and I couldn't really explain it. Still in shock, I tried my best to just walk him through my every action. After explaining it all to him, he finally says ok.

By now we have made it to the ER. We went through the now-familiar routine of check-in and waiting. This time, because I was further along in my pregnancy, the doctors conducted an ultrasound. The room was silent as the doctor moved the ultrasound wand over my belly, searching for signs of life. The silence was deafening, a prelude to the inevitable news. When the doctor finally spoke, his words confirmed my worst fears: my uterus was empty. "Empty"! I repeated, how could that be. I did not understand it. I had lost the baby, likely in that fleeting moment in the bathroom stall.

Replaying the moment in the stall over and over again in my head. I said, one minute I'm standing there pregnant and in a matter of seconds, I fill my baby slide right out of me. Before I can even grasp what just happened, the automatic flush whisks my baby away. I didn't have a moment to breathe, to think, to cry, or do anything, the baby was just gone. Bringing my mind back to the hospital room where my husband, the doctor, and the nurse were standing, I can tell they were waiting for and looking for a response from me. The news hit me like a tidal wave, a profound sorrow washing over me as I realized the gravity of what had happened.

The Role of Active Listening in Leadership

In moments of profound grief and confusion, like the one I experienced at the comedy show, the need for understanding and support is paramount. Active listening plays a critical role in providing this support. As a Leader, it is vital to create an environment where Soldiers feel safe to share their experiences, no matter how difficult or personal.

"Effective leadership begins with listening", once quoted by Major General Linda Singh. Although I did not have any interactions with my leaders in the moments leading up to that devasting outcome, I was able to talk about what happened with one of my leaders later. It was not easy to express everything, but that leader listened, and she was attentive. That was the support I needed during that period of my life. I did not need judgment nor a leader trying to explain, how they went through similar pregnancy challenges. Every individual is entitled to live out their own stories, not all are alike.

Active listening involves more than just hearing words; it requires being fully present, acknowledging the speaker's emotions, and responding with empathy and support. It means validating their feelings and experiences, offering a non-judgmental space for them to process and express their emotions.

For leaders in the military, this skill is crucial in helping Soldiers navigate the challenges of pregnancy, postpartum, and loss. These experiences can be isolating, and the stigma around discussing such personal matters can prevent Soldiers from seeking the help they need. By actively listening, leaders can break down these barriers, fostering a culture where openness and vulnerability are met with understanding and care.

Lessons Learned and Strength Gained

Standing alone in that bathroom stall, I felt a profound sense of helplessness. The experience continues to haunt me, a stark reminder of the fragility of life and the uncontrollable nature of certain events. However, it also underscored the importance of having a supportive and understanding partner, as my husband was there to rush me to the ER and stand by my side as we received the devastating news.

This chapter emphasizes that leaders can play a similar supportive role for their Soldiers. By listening actively and empathetically, leaders can provide a crucial lifeline, helping Soldiers feel less isolated in their grief and more connected to a supportive community.

As we continue through this blue book, remember that active listening is not just a skill but a commitment to understanding and supporting others. It is a powerful tool that can transform lives and build a culture of care within the military community.

> *"The greatest leaders are those who are able to listen and take in the wisdom and perspectives of others."*
>
> ~ General Colin Powell

03 / LESSON / 03

Lesson Three:
Recognizing the Signs - Early Detection of Emotional and Physical Struggles

Building a culture of care within the Army requires Leaders to be vigilant and proactive, especially when it comes to supporting Soldiers who are navigating the challenging period of pregnancy and postpartum. One of the most critical steps in this journey is recognizing the signs of emotional and physical struggles, such as postpartum depression, anxiety, and grief, which can significantly impact a soldier's well-being and readiness.

Postpartum depression and anxiety are not uncommon, yet they often go unnoticed or are misinterpreted as normal stressors of military life. The unique pressures faced by Soldiers—whether it's the anticipation of deployment, the strain of separation from family, or the rigors of physical training—can exacerbate these conditions. Leaders must be trained to identify the subtle and overt signs that a Soldier may be struggling.

Early Detection and Timely Support: The Role of Leadership

Leaders at all levels should be equipped with the knowledge to detect early signs of postpartum emotional and physical challenges. This begins with education. Training programs should be implemented to help Leaders understand the symptoms of postpartum depression and anxiety, which may include persistent sadness, overwhelming fatigue, irritability, changes in appetite or sleep patterns, and withdrawal from social interactions. Recognizing these signs early allows for timely intervention, potentially preventing more severe outcomes.

Additionally, grief is another emotional struggle that Leaders must be prepared to address. Pregnancy loss, stillbirth, or complications can lead to profound grief, which may manifest in various ways, including depression, anxiety, or a general decline in performance. Leaders must approach these situations with sensitivity and compassion, offering support without judgment.

A Personal Account: The Impact of Inadequate Support

I share this piece of my story because it was the most impactful pregnancy out of all of them that changed how I started to view life. It also changed how I started to see my life in the military because of my Leaders. Looking back, I don't blame any of them, nor my peers, but I wish there had been someone there coaching them on how to better support someone like me who had other pregnancy losses. I also recognize that had I not been so private about my personal life my Leaders would have known how to approach me and my situation being pregnant. More than anything, I wish my leaders had helped me to understand better and know how to cope with anxiety, grief, and postpartum. Leaders at all levels need to make these Soldiers still feel valuable and find alternate ways for them to contribute to the mission. They have to remember that they are carrying a life inside of them.

My personal story starts with the concluding ceremonies of one Basic Training Cycle at Fort Jackson, South Carolina. I was the Battalion Executive Officer, so because of my duty position and rank I had a responsibility to be on the center of the graduation field and leading the troops, about 1300 Soldiers at any given time to be exact. I was to take charge of the formation and lead them through drills as the "Commander of Troops" or COT. I was not nervous nor hesitant as I had done this duty several times before. What I hesitated about was taking the field in my current situation. I was pregnant and about 25 weeks and a few days along. I still presented a stellar appearance, even with a belly, and my commander had commended me several times before due to my hard work and dedication. So he had high expectations of me showing up for the mission, like many times before. What he did not know were my hidden scars from all of my previous pregnancies.

I found myself standing in his office a few days before the actual graduation ceremony discussing if I would lead the troops. I explained to him that I did not feel comfortable taking the field. At first, he questioned my hesitation, wondering if I just didn't want to do it or if my doctor had given me limitations. I had to explain to him that my doctor did not give me any limitations, but I knew my body and I did not think it was a good idea.

Some may fault the medical professional that I was in the care of, but due to my lengthy unforeseen pregnancy history and recent PCSs, my doctor only understood the extent of my pregnancy losses from reading my medical records. Even she didn't feel the need to give me limitations, but I knew my body.

After finally agreeing to a second coarse of action with my commander, I was relieved of my duty as the COT for that graduation. He ended up appointing a junior officer that would be taking over for me once I went on maternity leave in the near future. So I assisted that officer with rehearsing and preparing for the ceremony. On the day of the ceremony, I got to enjoy watching from the stadium seats.

I remember parking down the way from the stadium to avoid having to sit in family traffic at the conclusion of the ceremony. To me, the walk did not seem long. The weather was nice out, the sun was shinning. It seemed to be a great day to be having an outdoor ceremony. The stands were filled with over 3,000 Family Members coming to cheer on and support their new Soldier into the Army ranks. When the ceremony finally concluded, I hung around for a minute to thank my staff for putting things all together. I thanked the junior officer for standing in for me and complimented him on doing a great job on the field. Lastly, I said a few hellos to the Senior Leaders present to include my commander and his wife; the brigade command team; and the post command team and their spouses.

To me, this was a typical graduation ceremony day. Same ceremony, same protocols. After acknowledging them all, I decided to head home for the day, by now I was tired.

When I arrived home, all I wanted to do was grab a glass of water, kick off my boots and lay down; so that's what I did. After about an hour of dosing off, I started sneezing and that's what I remember waking me up. To my surprise, I also felt the urge to use the restroom. So I stood to my feet and before I could take my second step, I felt fluid gushing down my legs. This was something new. I had never had that much fluid come out of me before. So as I stood there in shock, the fluid continued to run and I yelled for my husband. He came rushing in and was just as surprised as I was.

Before I knew it, I was sitting on the floor because I didn't want to move any more. I urged him to call for an ambulance, as I was fearful I would start bleeding soon. When the paramedics finally arrived they lifted me onto the gurney and rolled me out our front door. On the way to the hospital they continued to check my vitals and everything remained normal.

When we finally made it to the hospital, the experience was nothing like I had experienced before. I remember them wheeling me in through a back door to the emergency room and taking me up to the maternity ward on an elevator. They explained to me that because I was so far along, I needed to go straight upstairs and not in the ER.

While at the hospital, I noticed the nurses did not move with a sense of urgency, both with my admissions process and with the NICU support team. In my short memoir titled "Partum my Silence", I go in to a bit more detail of my experience at the hospital and how the birth went. For the sake of the blue book I will restrain from telling my entire experience.

But within 24 hours of attending the graduation ceremony, I found myself in the hospital. My water had busted only hours after attending that ceremony and within the next 24hours the doctors were inducing me because I had started to acquire sepsis. Sepsis is a life-threatening condition that occurs when the body's response to an infection during pregnancy causes injury to it's own tissues and organs. In my case, it had started worsening and the doctors had to save my life or the baby's.

After the long hours of labor through the night, the baby was finally ready to come in the early morning. Aside from the sepsis, the delivery was successful. My baby boy survived for two hours before the NICU team had to finally call his time of death because after constant attempts he could not maintain his breathing on his own. His lungs were too underdeveloped.

The next 48 hours couldn't have been any more traumatic. After finally cleaning me all up, they transferred me to another maternity waiting room. This is where we rested until my vitals returned to normal and they approved me for discharge. While waiting in that room, several decisions had to be made for the remains of our son. We had to decide on funeral arrangements, it was dreadful to stomach so soon. As we made decisions and waited, the nurses brought the baby boy to the room in a bucket full of ice. They had dressed him and left him there on ice to reserve his remains.

I felt suffocated sitting in the hospital room. He remained there at the foot of my bed until we were discharged a day later. The memories I had in those moments could never escape my thoughts.

In the weeks and months that followed, I found myself lost, searching for something to fill the void. I remember buying a new car every month, unable to find contentment in my daily life. The signs were there, but I'm not sure I had Leaders paying attention. My actions were a cry for help, a manifestation of the deep grief and anxiety that I was struggling to manage alone.

I share this intimate story of mine to explain how traumatic some Soldiers pregnancies can be, but if they don't have the opportunity to express themselves, they can find themselves spiraling into a pull of depression. As leaders, don't think you are not able to help.

This next section is a helpful guide and some practical steps Leaders can implement to further connect with their postpartum Soldier.

Practical Steps for Leaders

1. *Active Observation:* Leaders should make a habit of actively observing their soldiers, paying close attention to changes in behavior, mood, and physical health. This includes noting any significant weight loss or gain, changes in demeanor, or an inability to focus on tasks. Uncharacteristic behavior, like sudden and frequent purchases, might also be a sign of deeper emotional struggles.

2. *Open Communication:* Establishing an environment where soldiers feel safe to express their concerns is crucial. Leaders should encourage open dialogue, where soldiers feel comfortable discussing their struggles without fear of stigma or repercussions.

3. *Regular Check-ins:* Implementing routine check-ins with Soldiers, particularly those who are pregnant or recently postpartum, can help Leaders stay attuned to any emerging issues. These check-ins should be conducted in a private, supportive manner to ensure Soldiers feel their concerns are heard.

4. *Referral to Professional Support:* When a leader identifies a soldier who may be struggling, it's essential to refer them to appropriate resources, such as mental health professionals, counselors, or support groups. Leaders should be familiar with the resources available within the military system and be prepared to assist in accessing these services.

By training leaders to recognize the signs of postpartum depression, anxiety, and grief, the Army can foster a culture of care that supports the holistic well-being of its soldiers. Early detection and intervention are key components in ensuring that Soldiers receive the help they need during one of the most vulnerable times in their lives.

> *Communities* and countries and ultimately *the world* are only as strong as the health of their women.

~ Michelle Obama

04 / LESSON / 04

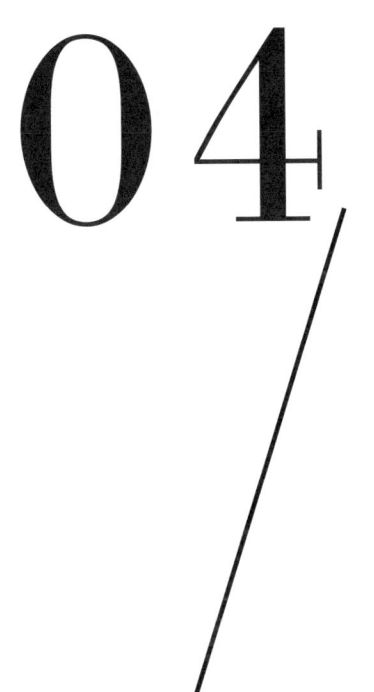

Lesson Four:
Supportive Policies - Implementing Family- Friendly Practices

Supporting Soldiers through pregnancy and postpartum requires more than just empathy; it demands the implementation of strong, family-friendly policies that accommodate the unique needs of these individuals. Policies that offer flexible leave, provide necessary accommodations, and recognize the physical and emotional demands of pregnancy are essential to creating a supportive environment. This chapter explores the importance of these policies, underscored by a personal experience that highlights the critical need to prioritize health over duty.

A Personal Experience: The Delta Company Change of Command

As a senior leader nearing the end of my military career, I found myself at a crossroads: preparing for a Permanent Change of Station (PCS) or getting ready to drop my retirement packet. During this time, I was serving as a Battalion Executive Officer at Fort Jackson, South Carolina. My responsibilities included overseeing various company-level activities, and on one occasion, I had to step in for my Battalion Commander, who was out of town on temporary duty (TDY).

A Delta Company Change of Command ceremony was scheduled, and it was my duty to officiate in the Battalion Commander's absence. This wasn't a new task for me; I had officiated many ceremonies throughout my career, and I felt confident in my ability to manage the event. We conducted several rehearsals outside under the barracks where the ceremony would take place. The practice was straightforward, and there was no undue stress involved.

However, as the rehearsals progressed, I began to feel a nagging pain in my lower back. At first, I tried to push through it, determined to complete one more rehearsal to ensure the outgoing commander felt confident in his role. After the final practice, I rushed to the restroom, half-way expecting to see blood. A fear that had lingered and I maintained since my previous losses. To my relief, there was none, and I felt a momentary sense of calm.

I returned to the office and sat on the couch in my Command

Sergeant Major's (CSM) office, trying to ease the discomfort in my back. I mentioned the pain to my CSM but assured him I was fine to continue with the ceremony. In my mind, I knew I had not seen any blood, so I didn't think anything bad was wrong. As I sat there in his office, the pain persisted, gnawing at my focus. Despite this, I convinced myself that the ceremony was paramount and that I could push through.

When the Brigade Commander and Brigade Command Sergeant Major arrived to our building, we headed out of CSM office and out toward the ceremony. As to not keep our higher command team waiting, I got up from the couch, mentally preparing myself for the task ahead. When we arrived outside, familiar with the set up, I immediately took my place for the event. The Change of Command ceremony went off without a hitch, just as we had practiced.

By the time it was over, I knew something wasn't right. The pain in my lower back had not subsided, and I felt an overwhelming sense of fatigue. I turned to my CSM and informed him that I needed to leave early. I told him that perhaps my body was signaling that it needed rest, and I could no longer ignore it. I went to my office, packed up my things, and headed home, where I promptly got into bed, trying to listen to what my body was telling me.

I did not rush off immediately to the hospital because of my past instances, they typically involved the sign of blood. This time was different, I did not have an immediate onset of bleeding, I was experiencing the pain though. So after about two days, I started to experience other signs. By the third day I went in to see my OBGYN and she conducted an ultrasound. They could not find a heartbeat. The undeniable loss had happened once again.

She explained to me that she could not identify a cause and I would just have to give it a couple more days because my body would dispel the remains on its own. Shocking as it was, it was not as hurtful as learning of the news from times before. By the next week, I reported into work. I explained to my commander what had happened after he returned from his TDY trip and he immediately told me to take a few days off. I took the time off to myself and came back to work when I felt I was ready.

The Importance of Supportive Policies

This experience taught me a critical lesson about the need for supportive policies that prioritize the health and well-being of Soldiers, particularly during pregnancy. In the military, there is often a relentless focus on the mission, and Soldiers may feel pressured to push through physical discomfort or emotional distress to fulfill their duties. However, this mindset can be detrimental, especially during pregnancy, when the health of both the mother and the baby are at stake.

Family-friendly policies, such as flexible leave and accommodations for pregnant Soldiers, are essential in fostering a supportive environment. These policies must be enforced consistently, ensuring that Soldiers feel empowered to prioritize their health without fear of repercussions. In my case, having the flexibility to leave early and rest was crucial in preventing further strain on my body.

Lessons Learned and Strength Gained

The lesson I learned from this experience is clear: Listen to your body, and advocate for policies that allow Soldiers to do the same. The mission will continue with or without you, but your health and the health of your baby are irreplaceable. By implementing and enforcing supportive policies, we can create a culture where Soldiers feel valued and supported, knowing that their well-being is a top priority.

As Leaders, it is our responsibility to ensure that these policies are in place and that they are communicated effectively to all Soldiers. COL Candis Martin once said, "leadership is not just about setting an example but also about creating policies that support and enable your team to thrive". By doing so, we can build a culture of care that supports Soldiers through all stages of life, including the challenges of pregnancy and postpartum. This is not just about accommodating individual needs; it's about creating a stronger, more resilient force that values the well-being of its members.

> *"A leader is one who knows the way, goes the way, and shows the way. Policies should reflect the path we want to follow."*

~ John C. Maxwell

05 / LESSON / 05

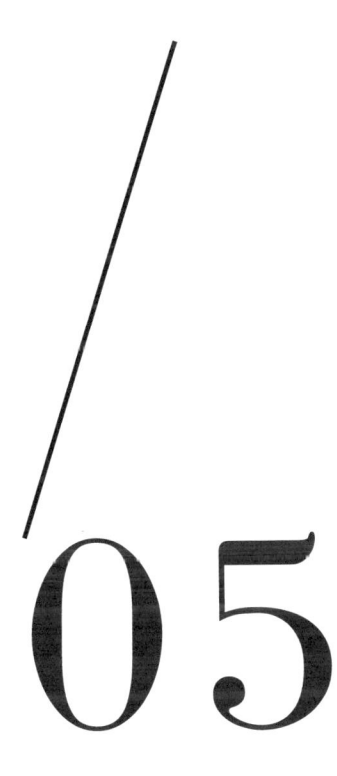

Lesson Five:
Resource Awareness - Connecting Soldiers with Professional Help

Resource awareness is a critical component of supporting Soldiers during pregnancy and postpartum. Leaders play a crucial role in ensuring that Soldiers are aware of, and connected to, the resources available to them. This chapter will explore how leaders can become knowledgeable about these resources, advocate for their Soldiers, and help them build a support network that extends beyond the military installation.

The Importance of Resource Awareness

Navigating pregnancy and postpartum as a Soldier comes with unique challenges. The physical demands of military life, coupled with the emotional toll of pregnancy and potential loss, require a strong support system. Leaders must be well-versed in the resources available to their Soldiers, from mental health services to medical care, and be prepared to guide them through these difficult times. MG Linda Singh once stated that "being aware of the resources at your disposal is crucial in guiding your team effectively and making informed decisions."

Resource awareness is not just about knowing what services exist; it's about understanding how to access them and ensuring that Soldiers feel supported in seeking the help they need.

Behavioral Health Resources within the Army

The Army provides a range of behavioral health resources aimed at supporting Soldiers' mental and emotional well-being. Behavioral health clinics on military installations offer counseling services, mental health care, and support groups specifically designed for military personnel. These resources are invaluable, especially for Soldiers dealing with the stress and trauma of pregnancy loss.

However, there are times when Soldiers may require additional support that goes beyond what is available on base. This is where Leaders can make a significant impact by encouraging Soldiers to seek external behavioral health counseling.

Advocating for External Behavioral Health Counseling

Leaders should support their Soldiers in advocating for external behavioral health counseling when necessary. This can be done through their primary care physician, who can provide referrals to civilian counselors or specialists. External counseling can offer a level of privacy and comfort that some Soldiers may prefer, especially if they are hesitant to seek help within the military system.

Encouraging Soldiers to advocate for their mental health is crucial. As a Leader, you can assist them in navigating the healthcare system, ensuring they understand their options, and empowering them to take control of their well-being.

Expanding Support Networks Beyond the Installation

In addition to the resources available on base, Soldiers can benefit from connecting with support networks in the local community. Local organizations often offer support groups, counseling services, and other resources that can provide Soldiers with additional layers of support.

Online platforms like Facebook also host a variety of support groups tailored to specific needs, such as pregnancy, postpartum, and grief. These groups can be a valuable resource for Soldiers seeking connection and understanding from others who have shared similar experiences.

My Personal Experience: Finding Hope in the Community

During my own experiences with pregnancy loss, I found that connecting with my local community was a source of immense support. As a Leader, I was in a position where I felt a strong responsibility to my Soldiers and my duties. The timing of my pregnancy losses and maternity leave made it challenging for me to go on the installation, so I sought solace elsewhere. I began taking walks around my local community, not with any destination in mind, but simply to clear my head. During these walks, I encountered individuals who, in ways both big and small, poured hope back into me. They weren't part of my military world, but they became part of my healing process.

They were there for me during some of the most challenging times of my life, and I will forever be grateful to my family, my friends, and my community for embracing me when I needed it most. This experience taught me the value of looking beyond the immediate environment for support. Sometimes, the help we need comes from unexpected places, and it's important for Soldiers to know that it's okay to seek support outside of the military framework.

The Role of Leaders in Connecting Soldiers with Resources

Leaders must be proactive in ensuring that their Soldiers are connected to the resources they need. This means being knowledgeable about the services available on base, but also recognizing when external resources might be more appropriate. It also involves encouraging Soldiers to take an active role in their own care and advocating for the support they need.

Fostering an environment where seeking help is normalized and encouraged is vital. By doing so, Leaders can help Soldiers feel empowered to pursue the resources that will best support their mental and emotional well-being.

Conclusion

Resource awareness is a key element in creating a culture of care for Soldiers during pregnancy and postpartum. By connecting Soldiers with both military and civilian resources, leaders can ensure that their Soldiers receive the comprehensive care they need. Encouraging Soldiers to advocate for themselves and to seek support beyond the installation can make all the difference in their journey toward healing and resilience. As Leaders, our role is to guide, support, and empower our Soldiers every step of the way.

> *"Leaders* who are aware of the resources available to them *are better* equipped to guide their teams effectively."

~ General George S. Patton

06 / LESSON / 06

Lesson Six:
Creating a Community: Fostering Peer Support Networks

One of the most powerful tools in helping Soldiers cope with the unique challenges of pregnancy and postpartum experiences, particularly after the loss of a child, is the establishment of peer support networks. These networks, whether formal or informal, can provide a sense of community, understanding, and shared experience that can be invaluable during difficult times. As leaders, it is our responsibility to not only encourage the development of these support networks but also to actively foster an environment where Soldiers feel comfortable seeking and offering support to one another.

The Power of Peer Support

Peer support networks create a space where Soldiers can share their experiences, emotions, and challenges without fear of judgment. The value of these networks cannot be overstated, as they offer a unique kind of support that is often different from what can be provided by medical professionals or even family members. Soldiers who have gone through similar experiences can offer insights, empathy, and a level of understanding that can help others navigate their own journeys.

In my experience, the Army does an excellent job in fostering this kind of community through established programs like Pregnancy Postpartum Physical Training (PPP PT). However, it's important to recognize that while these programs exist, their full potential is realized when leaders actively promote and participate in them.

Pregnancy Postpartum Physical Training (PPPPT)
PPP PT is a program designed to support Soldiers during pregnancy and postpartum, providing a tailored physical training environment that takes into account the unique needs of pregnant and postpartum Soldiers. In all my years in the Army, I had never attended a PPPPT session until my latter years of service. It was during this time that I truly came to appreciate the program's benefits.

For the first time, I found myself in an environment where I didn't have to put on the armor of being a senior leader who had it all together. I could focus on my own physical and emotional well-being, with my body and my baby in mind, without feeling the pressure to keep up with the demands of regular physical training. The other Soldiers I met during these sessions were much younger than me, but I enjoyed connecting with them and learning about pregnancy and motherhood together during some of the in-class instruction.

The Hard Truths

However, my experience in PPP PT also brought to light some of the hard truths that Soldiers face. In my conversations with a few of the younger Soldiers, I learned that they were in PPP PT not just because they were pregnant, but because they had recently miscarried or lost a child. These revelations were heartbreaking, and I felt helpless in those moments, not only because I had experienced losses before, but because I wondered if their leaders truly understood the depth of their pain and the highs and lows of their emotions.

It made me question whether these Soldiers were just "waved away" to PPP PT, without a full acknowledgment of their emotional and mental state. This is where peer support becomes crucial. While PPP PT provides a structured environment for physical recovery, it's the peer connections made within that space that often provide the emotional and psychological support needed to truly heal.

7 LEADERSHIP LESSONS

Fostering a Culture of Peer Support

Leaders must go beyond simply directing Soldiers to programs like PPP PT. We must actively engage with these programs, encourage participation, and ensure that Soldiers know they have a network of peers who understand and support them. Creating a culture of peer support requires leaders to be visible, approachable, and willing to share their own experiences, as appropriate, to build trust and encourage openness.

We should also advocate for additional support mechanisms, such as peer mentoring programs, where more experienced Soldiers who have gone through similar challenges can offer guidance and support to those who are just beginning their journeys. This can be particularly effective for Soldiers who may feel isolated or reluctant to share their struggles in a more formal setting.

Conclusion

The importance of peer support networks in helping Soldiers cope with the challenges of pregnancy and postpartum cannot be underestimated. As leaders, we have the ability to foster these networks, ensuring that Soldiers have the support they need not only to recover physically but also to heal emotionally and mentally. Programs like PPP PT are a great start, but it's up to us to create a culture where Soldiers feel truly supported by their peers, where they can share their experiences without fear of judgment, and where they can find strength in the shared experience of others.

"The strength of the team is each individual member. The strength of each member is the team."

~ Phil Jackson

07 / LESSON / 07

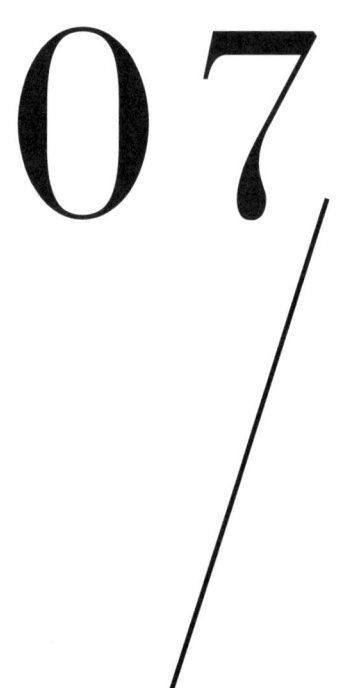

Lesson Seven:
Continual Education: Ongoing Training and Development for Leaders

As Leaders in the Army, our responsibilities extend far beyond mission accomplishment and maintaining readiness. We are entrusted with the well-being of our Soldiers, and this includes understanding the complexities of their lives, especially when it comes to pregnancy, postpartum challenges, and the trauma of losing a child.

This final lesson underscores the importance of ongoing education and training for Leaders. MG Singh stated, "education is a lifelong journey". It's not just about knowing the regulations or the standard operating procedures; it's about being equipped to handle the emotional and psychological challenges that our Soldiers face. We must be committed to continual learning and growth, both for our sake and for those we lead it ensures as Leaders we stay relevant and effective.

In my 20-plus years of service, I've seen firsthand the gaps in understanding and empathy that can exist within our ranks. I've been pregnant six times, and out of those pregnancies, I have two living children. I've also experienced three miscarriages and the devastating loss of a son who lived for only two hours after being born prematurely. These experiences have shaped who I am today and have given me a deep understanding of the struggles that pregnant Soldiers and those who have lost a child endure.

As a retired combat veteran who has deployed three times, I know the pressures that come with leadership in the Army. I understand the demands of the mission and the weight of responsibility that we carry. But I also know that we must never forget that our Soldiers are human beings with lives, families, and emotions. The lessons I've learned through my own experiences are invaluable, and I believe they can contribute to changing the culture of how Army Leaders care for Soldiers who may feel unseen or misunderstood.

To be truly effective Leaders, we must commit to continual education and development. This includes attending workshops, seeking out resources, and engaging in discussions about the emotional and mental health challenges that our Soldiers face. It also means being willing to learn from those who have walked the path before us. Now that I am retired, I feel a deep calling to offer my services back to the military community. I want to help bridge the gap between Leaders and Soldiers, especially when it comes to understanding and supporting those who are dealing with pregnancy and loss. My journey has given me unique insights, and I believe that by sharing my experiences and knowledge, I can help other leaders become more compassionate, empathetic, and effective.

Let this chapter be a call to action for all leaders. We must hold ourselves accountable for the well-being of our Soldiers. We must ensure that we are continually learning, growing, and evolving as Leaders. And we must strive to create an environment where every Soldier feels seen, heard, and supported, no matter what challenges they are facing.

The lessons I've shared in this book are not just for the Soldiers who are going through difficult times; they are for the leaders who have the power to make a difference in their lives. Let's commit to being the kind of Leaders who make that difference. Let's ensure that no Soldier ever feels alone in their journey, and that they know they have a Leader who truly understands and cares.

> "*When you've worked* hard, and done well, and walked through that *doorway of opportunity* you do not slam it shut behind you. *You reach back.*"

~ Michelle Obama

FINAL REFLECTIONS

Final Reflections

The thoughts and examples I have shared throughout this book have been nesting in my mind and heart for quite some time. These reflections have taken shape through the experiences that marked my journey as both a Soldier and a mother, and I am glad you have taken the time to walk with me through these personal stories. More importantly, I hope you find the lessons shared here to be not just helpful but transformative for your role as a leader and for the culture of care within your organization.

The journey to motherhood while serving in the Army was, for me, filled with both profound loss and immeasurable joy. While I have focused on the most traumatic experiences, such as my miscarriages and the loss of my son, I want to acknowledge the moments of triumph as well. The Lord blessed me with two healthy, growing, and thriving little boys who are the light of my life. These successful pregnancies remind me that even amidst sorrow, there is hope and new beginnings.

My journey was marked by moments of uncertainty and medical challenges. My first two pregnancies ended early, and the losses were documented as "unexplained miscarriages." After these losses, I was referred to maternal-fetal medicine specialists who carefully monitored me to uncover the underlying issues. By my third pregnancy, doctors identified an incompetent cervix as a potential cause of the previous losses. With this knowledge, precautionary steps were taken to ensure the success of my third pregnancy. Though my son was born a few weeks early, he arrived healthy, and we overcame the minor complications that followed his birth.

The road was not without further heartache. My fourth pregnancy also ended early as an unexplained miscarriage. By the time I learned I was pregnant for the fifth time, I was emotionally exhausted. My mind, body, and spirit had endured so much loss that I struggled to find excitement in the news. I approached the pregnancy with caution, focusing instead on cherishing the time with my then two-year-old son. Tragically, my baby boy was born at just 25 weeks, and despite the NICU team's efforts, they could not save his life.

When I became pregnant for the sixth time, my husband and I seriously considered taking steps to prevent any future pregnancies. We were both exhausted, not just physically, but emotionally as well. We had stopped "trying" to have children after our second son was born, simply trying to enjoy the romantic side of our marriage. Yet, life had other plans. Baby number six was our last, and this pregnancy proved to be a turning point. My son stayed in my womb for the full 42 weeks, the longest of any of my pregnancies. I attribute this to a sense of peace and calmness that I embraced throughout the pregnancy. I carried him without any specific expectations, simply focusing on staying in a state of serenity. He is now here with us, a joyful and peaceful child.

Each of these pregnancies, whether marked by loss or life, contributed to the person and leader I have become. These experiences were not just about the physical challenges of pregnancy but about resilience, growth, and leadership at every level of my career. Each step of this journey provided me with different experiences, each one shaping me into a stronger leader. This is why compiling this "Leader's Blue Book" was so important to me.

As I reflect on these experiences and the seven powerful lessons I have shared, I am reminded of the importance of creating a culture of care within the Army. Leaders must be equipped not just with knowledge but with empathy, understanding, and the ability to advocate for their Soldiers. The experiences I have shared are more than just stories—they are lessons in resilience, in the strength of community, and in the power of compassionate leadership.

It is my hope that this book serves as a guide for leaders who are navigating the complexities of supporting Soldiers through pregnancy and postpartum experiences. The challenges are real, and the pain is deep, but with the right support, we can create an environment where Soldiers feel seen, understood, and cared for. In doing so, we build a stronger, more resilient force, capable of not just enduring but thriving through the trials that life inevitably brings.

ABOUT THE AUTHOR

About the Author

Coraetta Andrena is a proud native of New Orleans, Louisiana. Growing up as her mother's only daughter, Coraetta faced the challenges of losing her father at a young age and being raised by a single mother alongside her two brothers. She is the only one of her siblings to join the U.S. Army, where she embarked on an extraordinary journey that spanned 20.5 years and took her to the frontlines of Iraq and Afghanistan in support of Operation Iraqi Freedom and Operation Enduring Freedom.

Coraetta began her military career as a Private First Class (PFC) assigned to the 35th Signal Brigade at Fort Bragg, North Carolina. Her journey then took her to Dexheim, Germany, where she served as the CLIX Warehouse NCOIC with the 123rd Main Support Brigade. After her tour in Germany, she pursued her goal of becoming a commissioned officer, achieving the rank of First Lieutenant (1LT) in 2009. As an officer, she held various key positions, including her first assignment with the 226th Quartermaster Company at Fort Stewart, Georgia. She then served in the G4 Directorate of 8th Army in Seoul, South Korea, before moving to Fort Polk, Louisiana, where she commanded the Alpha Distribution Company of the 710th

Brigade Support Battalion, responsible for providing logistical support to the 3rd Infantry Brigade Combat Team.

Her distinguished career continued as she became an Assistant Professor of Military Science at Loyola University and Towson University in Maryland. She concluded her military service at Fort Jackson, South Carolina, serving as the Battalion Executive Officer of the 3/60th Basic Combat Training Battalion.

Coraetta's commitment to excellence is further reflected in her academic achievements. She holds a Bachelor of Science in Psychology from Kansas State University and a Master's degree in Business Management with a concentration in Logistics from the Florida Institute of Technology.

Her military education is extensive, including Non-Commissioned Officer (NCO) training in the former Warrior Leaders Course (WLC) and Basic Non-Commissioned Officer Course (BNOC). As an officer, she completed Officer Candidate School, Quartermaster Basic Officer Leaders Course (BOLC), Combined Logistics Captain Career Course (CLC3), Command & General Staff College (Non-Resident), Support Operations Leaders Course (SPO), Equal Opportunity Leaders Course, Technical Transportation of Hazardous Materials, Sling Load Inspector Course, Recruiting Operations Course, and the

Foundation Instructor/Facilitator Course (FIFC). Throughout her military career, Coraetta earned numerous accolades, including two Meritorious Service Medals, the Bronze Star Medal, the Army Commendation Medal- Remote, and three Army Commendation Medals, four Army Achievement Medals, Meritorious Unit Commendation, four Army Good Conduct Medals, Global War on Terrorism Expeditionary Medal, Global War on Terrorism Service Medal, Korea Defense Service Medal, Afghanistan Campaign Medal w/ Campaign Star, Armed Forces Service Medal, Iraq Campaign Medal w/ two Campaign Stars, two Non Commissioned Officer Professional Development Ribbons, four Overseas Service Ribbons, and NATO Medal. She also holds an International Society of Logistics (SOLE) Demonstrated Senior Logistician Certification for all her years of technical training and experience.

In addition to her military accomplishments, Coraetta is a proud member of Zeta Phi Beta Sorority, Incorporated, where she continues to serve her community with the same dedication and passion that defined her military service.

Now retired from the military, Coraetta dedicates her life to pursuing her business goals, raising her two sons, Mark Jr. and Ca'Mari, and advocating for Soldiers in the Army experiencing postpartum challenges. She resides in Columbia, South Carolina, where she also cares for her twin nephews, Darryl and Darron, as they prepare for college.

Passionate about caring for others and offering unwavering support, Coraetta continues to be a beacon of strength and compassion in her community.

CITED QUOTATIONS

General Ann E. Dunwoody:

referenced in interviews, speeches, or her book:

- Dunwoody, Ann E. A Higher Standard: Leadership Strategies from America's First Female Four-Star General. Da Capo Press, 2015.

Major General Linda Singh:

found in her public speeches, interviews, and writings:

- Singh, Linda. Moments of Choice: My Path to Leadership. Self-published, 2018.

General Lori Robinson:

found in several interviews and profiles:

- "General Lori Robinson: The First Woman to Head a Major Unified Combatant Command." Time Magazine, various issues.

Colonel Candis Martin:

referenced in military publications and interviews.

Additional Resources

Here are some community outreach programs that can assist Army Leaders in developing their postpartum care campaigns:

Veterans Affairs (VA) Support Programs:
- Partner with local VA offices to access programs and resources specifically designed for postpartum care, including counseling, support groups, and health services.

Army Community Service (ACS):
- Collaborate with ACS to offer workshops and seminars on postpartum care, mental health, and wellness, tailored to the unique needs of military families.

Nonprofit Organizations:
- Engage with nonprofits like the National Military Family Association (NMFA) or Military One Source, which provide resources and support for postpartum care and can offer educational materials and support services.

Local Health Clinics:
- Partner with local health clinics or maternal health organizations to provide specialized care, health screenings, and postpartum support services for Soldiers and their families.

Support Groups and Peer Networks (3P PT):
- Establish or join existing support groups for postpartum soldiers, which can offer peer-to-peer support, share experiences, and provide a network of understanding individuals. Social Media Groups are another great resource.

Educational Institutions:
- Collaborate with universities or training institutes that offer programs in psychology, counseling, or social work to provide educational seminars or workshops on postpartum care.

To all the Soldiers—past, present, and future
—who have faced or will face the trials of pregnancy and loss while serving our country. No day is easier than the next after a loss, but it's essential to find strength in your sorrow. Someone is counting on you to show up, even if that someone is you. Your resilience and courage are a beacon of hope, and I dedicate this book to your journey, your healing, and your strength.

Made in the USA
Columbia, SC
26 September 2024